THE PARTY

How to have fun while finding true love

Written by

Terri Hanauer

Bambaz Press
Los Angeles 2024

ISBN: 979-8-8692-8724-3
© 2024 Terri Hanauer
All Rights Reserved

Cover Artwork: Celine Diano
Book Layout: Baz Here

Bambaz Press
Los Angeles, CA

"*The Party* is priceless...and it sets you up in a win-win situation. If you're sick of all the other ways to meet someone, you can't afford NOT to read this one!"

L.J.

"I was tired of online dating and getting scammed! *The Party* was the perfect solution."

P.L.

"Warm and witty, compassionate and insightful, the author's generosity of spirit can be felt on every page."

C.E.

"Trying to find a partner in a social media-driven world left me feeling deflated and disconnected. After reading *The Party* my confidence grew and I was ready to put myself out into the world again. I called the man I was crushing on and we've been together ever since. If it wasn't for *The Party* I wouldn't have had the courage to make the first move! I recommend this book without any hesitation. Love is patient. Love is kind. Love is FUN….and so is *The Party*."

A.A.

"For once, instead of just presenting (or complaining about) the problem, *The Party* actually offers a solution. Hanauer mixes experience with empathy. Her readers will appreciate her tender, humorous approach as it cuts to the chase. She clearly has her readers' best interests at heart. Brava! Nothing like a fresh, new voice!"

L. T.

"I had such a wonderful time. *The Party* was so well planned, I knew I was in good hands the whole evening. One of the best nights, ever! I would buy shares in the company."

M. L.

"A highly insightful, yet down to earth book that looks at the realities of today's dating experiences and offers a way for readers to meet new people who share their sensibilities and desires."

A. H.

"My friend told me about *The Party* and I thought I'd be too shy to get involved with it. She convinced me to help plan it and I'm glad I did. I actually met some cool guys that night. I didn't find the love of my life, but someone else I know is going to do another one. Really, it is helping me with my shyness. So I'm gonna go to the next one too."

R. A.

"Great read. Good advice. Funny anecdotes. I recommend it highly."

B. A.

"What can I say? I loved this book. I threw a party and it really helped me get off the rollercoaster of Internet dating. I mean, what do you have to lose? Try it and you'll never look back. Like me!"

J. A.

Some people feel the rain. Others just get wet.

–Bob Marley

Chapters

Recipes

$\heartsuit$

1. That night in Venice...

I was at a party in Venice, California. It was one of those parties—you know—cool looking people, delicious food, trendy music—and maybe, just maybe the love of my life would be there too. He'd notice me, smile, walk over and say something so charming I'd fall for him and that would be that—the beginning of true love.

Instead, I was sitting on a couch with three other women, all thinking that very same thought. How did I know we were thinking that very same thought? Because that's what you thought if you were at a party in Venice, or any other place, for that matter. It's basically why we went to parties, or clubs or even concerts. We were interested in the actual event we were attending, of course, but we were also secretly hoping the Angel of Romance would be there too, looking out for us.

Love is what everyone wants. What everyone deserves, right? Right!

So, there we were, maybe thirty of us—twenty women and ten men— talking mostly to the friends we came with, just like in high school. I believe we basically see love with the same eyes we looked through when we were teenagers. And it doesn't matter what decade you were a teenager. What does matter is how you felt about yourself as you experienced those impressionable, impactful, life-altering events that were the "firsts"– first kiss, first crush, first passion, first sex, first relationship, first heartbreak and first recovery. Because like it or not, that's what you still carry with you.

And then some of us experience more "firsts" years later. That evening, I was on my own for the first time after a ten-year marriage. I had a four-year-old son. My ex and I had a civil marriage and, therefore, an equally civil divorce. He was already on his way to his next wife. Meanwhile, I was working as an actress and photographer in Los Angeles, co-raising our son, and looking for someone I could love and who could love us. And so, there I was, at this party in Venice.

On my second wine spritzer, I separated myself from the party-goers and scanned the room. I observed intelligent, attractive women and men—late 20s to early 40s—in small groups, three to four people per pod. They were talking and moving to the rhythm of the music—but no one was acting on the real reason they were there.

If only someone like Dr. Ruth (Westheimer) or Oprah - either a love/sex therapist or a motivational celebrity, was here too, I thought. Either one would have the insight and courage to say out loud, "Hey there! I know why you're at this party. You want to meet new people. You want to find that special someone who was made for you, who really appreciates you, and who even falls in love with you. That's why you're here, right?" And in my fantasy, I heard everyone at the party shout back, "Right!"

The other element that was missing from this very cool soirée was fun. We were too busy hiding how nervous and self-conscious we felt. But this was pretty much how I felt at most parties. Getting ready for the party was more fun than being at the party itself.

So, when I left, I vowed to throw a party that would be different. One that would include fun, laughter and play coupled with the empowering intentionality of Dr. Ruth and Oprah.

And that's what I did.

Fast forward to the present. A few months ago, I was at my friend, Celeste's, 40th birthday party. I sat beside her friend, Francine, who was complaining that it was impossible to "meet guys in LA," especially since Covid. She had tried online dating and apps but found the experiences nerve-wracking and ultimately disappointing.

"Throw your own singles party," I suggested.

She said she wouldn't know where to begin. So, I told her about the ones I had thrown with some friends.

"Please throw another one," she said. "I promise I'll come."

Then I said, "You know, I'll do something better. I'll write a book about it—a guidebook on how to do it—so you can throw one yourself."

This is that book.

So, if you're twenty-one and just out of college or thirty-two and ready to meet someone or forty-three and fresh out of a marriage or fifty-four and tired of being on your own or sixty-five and coming out of a gray divorce or seventy-six and a widow, The Party is for everyone who wants to find true love and have fun while doing it.

FYI, I've changed names to protect people's privacy because everything I write about really happened.

♡

2. Remember fun?

When was the last time you had fun? The kind of fun that makes you feel alive, vibrant and joyful. The kind of fun that lets you experience the best parts of yourself and others. The kind of fun that washes away the blues and bouts of loneliness we all experience from time to time.

For me, fun is an occurrence of pure delight where I laugh freely and joyfully. It's the genuine enjoyment of pleasure. My friend, Brigitte, was recently working as the production designer on a feature film. She went to Belgium to finish up shooting. She said she had a great time because she was with a European crew that laughed all the time. She told me she hadn't laughed like that since she was a child in France. And then Brigitte realized laughter was sorely lacking in her life. That's when she decided to actively look for colleagues who were more open and fun to be with.

When you're laughing, you're most likely having fun. Have you noticed how often children laugh compared to adults? I thought about this and decided to conduct my own survey. I went to a few parks and sat near the playgrounds. At each one, I counted an average of ten laughs per minute. When I spent the same amount of time in restaurants filled with adult customers, I counted two laughs per minute. Not really a scientific study, but for me, it was conclusive. As adults, we simply don't laugh as much as we could and certainly not as much as we used to. And if fun doesn't exist without laughter, then adults are simply not having enough fun.

I love the feeling of laughter in my body. My heart speeds up, my mind is totally focused on the present experience, my facial expressions are joyous and attractive, and my sounds are light, playful and contagious. It's that contagious element of laughter I like the most. Try not to laugh when you're near someone who is laughing. It's almost impossible. Laughter is attractive on everyone, which is why being at a party where the main goal is fun creates an ideal place to connect with others.

My husband and children make me laugh. My friends make me laugh. I make me laugh. *I Love Lucy* reruns make me laugh. Chris Rock, Jimmy Kimmel and Amy Schumer make me laugh. *Love Actually, Death at a Funeral* and *The Lost City* make me laugh. Laughter is one of the reasons we crave entertainment. Just think for a second about what makes you laugh and how you feel when you're laughing. That's what I'm talking about!

Fun also involves play. Remember when we were kids and were told to go out and play? It was an order. Too bad we aren't given that order as adults.

I've worked as an actor, magician's assistant, photographer, director and writer. I think I became an artist at a very young age because my make-believe activities, like coming up with plays, helped me escape a very strict upbringing. I pretended to be fairytale characters. I had tea parties and fought galactic battles. I read fantasy, romance and mystery novels. One way I survived the restrictions of a highly structured childhood was to let my imagination run free.

I've noticed that the "play" aspect in a person's life seems to diminish in direct proportion to their age. As George Bernard Shaw famously said, "We don't stop playing because we grow old; we grow old because we stop playing."

Finland and China have adult playgrounds where seniors can go on swings that are built especially for them; where two friends who are in their 60s can sit on a teeter totter and have as much fun as 6-year-olds;

where sandboxes are bigger and therefore an invitation to a 70-year-old to make a sandcastle. My vote is for every city in the world to have adult playgrounds so we can all jump into our younger selves.

When we get together with others, the possibility of fun and play exists. Taking part in activities you like increases the body's serotonin. Stress goes away. Your complexion improves, your eyes shine, your energy goes from negative to positive and your libido gets stronger. You basically become that much more attractive and vital. You become the YOU that you were meant to be.

So, let's have fun. Let's laugh. Let's play. And let's find our true loves.

3. Why a party?

Why throw a party when it's easier to go online or on a dating app? It takes no effort to swipe left or right. You'll "meet" a guy. He's definitely cute. His texts are funny—short and to the point. He's got a dry sense of humor and supports humanitarian causes. And he loves animals. He's saved numerous dogs from kill-shelters. He must be a truly kind and compassionate guy. Yeah, right. And while we're on the topic, is your information on the dating app a true reflection of who you are?

Dating apps are so often the land of illusion and delusion. How many of you know people who've been lied to on these sites? Maybe you're one of them. The Internet has opened doors to all sorts of possibilities—positive and negative.

There's nothing really personal about online dating—which is what dating and getting to know someone ought to be. It's also like a buffet table—you're never really satisfied with what's on your plate, always anxious to go back for more food even if you're not hungry.

A friend of mine, Tessa, 28, had a date with a man she met on Tinder - if a ten-minute meeting at a bar can be considered a date because when ten minutes were up, he said he had an appointment to go to. As he was leaving, she saw him pull out his cell and click on Tinder. So, she figured she'd do the same.

Tessa is still meeting guys this way. She thinks that the next Tinder date will be better than the one she is currently having a drink with. It has become an addiction. Fear Of Missing Out—the constant fear that others might be having more fun than you. It's a social anxiety that perpetuates the dread that you made the wrong decision on how to spend your time. It keeps you glued to what others are doing on social media.

Sound familiar? My friend Hannah, 32, has a fear of missing out. No matter where she is—a fantastic café or fashionable boutique—she worries there's a more fantastic café or trendier boutique where she should be instead. She ends up being stressed out and unhappy rather than enjoying wherever she is at that moment.

A couple of girlfriends, Danielle, 36, and Chloe, 40, tried a speed-dating event. The women sat in a long row while the men moved from seat to seat, kind of like musical chairs. They had about four minutes to ask and answer questions as deep as, "What's your vision of happiness?" and "Describe your perfect companion." They judged and were judged simultaneously.

Danielle said, "It was like I was put on display, directly competing with my friend. I felt like a toy vying with other toys for the attention of men I didn't even like." She felt the whole experience was demeaning.

I was at a Starbucks, waiting in line for my Earl Grey tea, when I looked over at a guy on the "Coffee meets Bagel" dating app. He was setting up a date when all around him were attractive, most likely single women, on their phones, probably setting up dates as well. Not one of them looked up to connect with the person standing right next to them. I mean, crazy, right?

Phones have become shields. As long as you're on your phone, you're occupied. You're in control. But take that phone away, and you become vulnerable, open, uncomfortable and definitely not in control anymore. By looking up instead of down at your device, you immediately jump back into the world. Try it. Smile at the guy next to you at Starbucks. You never know, he just may smile back. And if he doesn't, who cares, because you're going to host a Party!

$\heartsuit$

4. The Party

I started thinking about what was missing at social events, AI setups, Internet dating sites and apps. Why was there usually a feeling of depression and hopelessness directly following a singles get together? Why was Internet dating so humiliating? Why were Tinder and Bumble like playing roulette with a possible serial killer? Why was it still so difficult to meet people?

And if you happened to be one of the rare few who did meet someone at a bar, then what about the next date or the date after? Was it really a date or was it a hook up? Why was it always a hot mess of confusing crossed wires? Why were you ghosted—that awful feeling when the guy you've had a seemingly great rapport with suddenly stops responding and totally disappears? Has he met someone else? Did you say something wrong? I think we've all been ghosted or done some ghosting ourselves because it's extremely difficult to tell someone you're not interested in them. It's easier to delete their texts and calls, hoping they'll get the hint. Ghosting hurts. It damages trust and vulnerability. And what about the vengeful online search into his history? And then the spiraling into negative feelings about yourself and the vow to never date again. Been there, done that.

One observation I had from the Venice party was that friends who came together usually stayed together and left together. No one actively stepped out of their comfort zone to meet someone new. It reminded me of my very first dance in 9th grade. The boys stayed on one side of the gym and the girls stayed on the other. How vulnerable I was—how vulnerable we all were—so insecure and impressionable, so naïve and hopeful. My friend Lacey confessed that she still feels this way whenever she goes to a party, and she's 42!

So how was my party going to be different? How was it going to become The Party? I came up with three ideas:

The first idea and perhaps the most important concept that came to me was that The Party would invite guests in a very unique way.

If a woman were invited, she would have to bring a guy with her. That's weird, you're probably thinking. Why bring a date to a singles party? Well, here's the novel idea. The guy wouldn't be a date. Instead, he'd be a platonic friend, a good buddy, someone Anne, for example, knew and liked.

The second idea was that this friend, let's call him Richard, had to be open to meeting a potential partner. He had to be honest and up front about wanting a relationship.

Okay—so the woman, Anne, brings Richard, who is open to finding a relationship. Perfect. Now what?

Here's the third idea. Richard invites another person - a woman, Cassie, who is his platonic friend, and who is also interested in finding true love. And then Cassie must bring a friend to the party as well. You guessed it—a male friend, Daniel.

THE LINK EFFECT

The Link Effect is based on the following three ideas that form the central premise of The Party.

1. A female guest brings a platonic male friend

2. who wants to find true love, and

3. he brings a platonic female friend who wants the same.

Imagine a link on a bracelet that connects to another link that connects to another link that eventually makes up the whole bracelet. That is The Link Effect.

Each guest comes with someone of the opposite sex they know and like. This way, they are not alone. This way, they don't stick with the person they brought. They get involved with the other guests who are in the exact same position.

The Link Effect creates an even number of men and women—unlike most parties where women outnumber men four to one. Everybody can throw a Party. The Link Effect applies if you're straight or LGBTQ+.

I had breakfast with a gay friend, Everly, who is 38, single and bewildered by the dating scene. She told me she organized a dinner party where she asked women she knew to bring some friends. It turned out the group was an extension of people she already knew. In other words, no one was actually someone she didn't know or hadn't heard about. Everyone was familiar with everyone, so the dinner party turned out to be a disappointment in the "finding true love" arena.

The Party opens up the possibility of meeting people who are outside your small world. Usually, it's the same old, same old when it's the same group attending the same get-togethers. For example, living in LA means lots of industry parties, which means the same types of people you already know (some you like and some you don't). By opening up the guest possibilities with The Link Effect, you step into new worlds of people and experiences. And let's face it, seeing only the same crowd over time is like living in a fishbowl where everyone knows everything about everybody. Opportunities for finding love become more and more limited.

Here's what happened when I threw the first Party with a couple of girlfriends, Jessica and Gigi. This is how The Link Effect worked.

Jessica told her married sister, Cora, about The Party. Cora's husband had a partner who worked in his law firm who was interested in coming. So, Jessica brought her brother-in-law's law partner, Travis. Travis invited his trainer, Miranda and she brought her friend, Jackson.

Gigi brought her buddy, Enrico. Enrico brought a friend from work, Ophelia. Ophelia told her cousin, Jonathan, who came and brought his neighbor Elizabeth who invited her dentist, Edward, to come. Edward invited his cousin, Alexa.

I invited my actor friend, Sebastian. He brought his twin sister, Margarite. She asked her accountant, Murray. He invited his chiropractor, Natasha.

Each one of the hosts invited five single friends. With The Link Effect, you can see how quickly and exponentially the guest list grew. As long as each person brought a friend of the opposite sex, who then also brought a friend of the opposite sex, the opportunities were endless. Some guests only brought one friend. That was totally fine. Others brought more.

*Expand your possibilities
by expanding your reach.*

$\heartsuit$

5. Me, throw a singles party?

If you're feeling overwhelmed at the thought of throwing a singles party, don't worry. Chapter 16 (page 90) is dedicated to taking you through the simple steps for throwing The Party by providing you with thorough directions for BEFORE, DURING and AFTER The Party. Easy and fun, I promise.

After being single, married, divorced and happily re-married, I'd like to share some thoughts, stories and advice inspired by The Party.

FIRST THINGS FIRST... CONFIDENCE

Sometimes, when my confidence is shaky, I follow the suggestion of one of my acting teachers. "Behave as if you are confident."

I discovered that by acting as if I were confident, I genuinely became more confident. This was certainly true in auditions. I'd talk to myself in the rear-view mirror of my car before going into the casting office. I'd look at my reflection and say, "You are loved. I have faith in you. You are talented and perfect for this part. Go in there and do your best. You are loved."

Then I'd walk what seemed like miles to the production office where I'd sit with other actresses up for the same role. I'd do my best at the audition. Then I'd leave, knowing that I had to let it all go because, at that point, I had no control over the outcome. I'd look to see if there was anything I could learn from the audition. Then I'd tuck that information away for the next time, and I'd move on with my life. Over the years, I've tried to perfect this way of being and thinking. Of course, sometimes I'd be a wreck for several days waiting to find out if I got the part. At other times, I'd forget about the audition and then my agent would call to tell me the role was mine. Either way, I tried to do my best so I could feel good about my work. I acted confident even when I was shaking on the inside. And isn't that where confidence starts? Having faith in yourself? So be confident, know you are loved and decide to throw The Party, and by all means, have fun doing it!

A DATE

Pick a date. That sounds so simple because it is. Ask any time management consultant or life coach who helps clients achieve goals. They'll tell them to pick a date of completion and work towards it.

Choose a Saturday night at least two months in the future. That will give you plenty of time.

CO-HOSTS

Make a list of your friends who are open and positive. It's always more fun if like-minded people are involved. Three co-hosts worked for us.

I recently spoke to my friend, Jessica, who co-hosted the first party with me. She reminded me that an acquaintance of hers, Lily, asked her to help throw The Party at her condo a couple of months after she'd been to ours. Jessica said yes and co-hosted Lily's Party with her. As Jessica was leaving, a handsome man who had just arrived said, "Where are you going? I just got here." They talked and made plans to see each other again, and again and again. Jessica and Harrison married and have been happily together ever since.

The other way to go is to hire The Party Party Planners. They are carefully chosen associates who can help you organize and throw The Party. They offer a number of packages that will fit every budget.

Check them out on the website: ThePartyTheBook.com

GUESTS

As I mentioned, I hosted the first Party with two friends. The three of us made a list of people we thought were interested in finding true love. We called them and explained the concept. Their response was a rousing, "Yes!"

VENUE

Decide on the venue for The Party. Pick a place that's comfortable and easy to get to. I had the party at my place. I was living in Santa Monica in a small two-bedroom Spanish style house. A party room in a condo complex works well. Someone's backyard, a neighborhood park, etc. Be creative.

Keeping safe and healthy is an optimal goal for any gathering these days. If you live in a warm climate, The Party can be held outdoors. If not, remember to make sure that the venue is well-ventilated.

INVITATIONS

Here are a few examples of invitations for The Party. Feel free to come up with your own. Make sure to include that their plus one needs to be of the opposite sex. It ensures an even number of men and women. The wider the chain grows, the more opportunities of intentionally meeting and connecting with others. Include an age range if that's important to you. Here are sample invitations:

Dear Jasper,

I'm co-hosting a Party on Saturday February 13th. It's a party to give people a chance to meet someone they'd be interested in dating and getting to know.

Please come with a guest who is a female friend of yours. That guest should be a woman you are friends with but aren't in a romantic relationship with. Then ask her to invite a guy she's just friends with. Ages 25 - 35, please. That's it!

Location: My house

Time: 8:00

Women - bring a dish

Men - bring something to drink

RSVP either way. Please call to find out more about The Party.

Thanks, and get ready to have fun!

Yours,

____

Hey Teresa!

I'm co-hosting a Party where people will have fun finding true love. Please join us.

If you want to come, bring a single, platonic male friend as your guest. And ask him to bring a platonic female friend.

Men – please bring something to eat

Women – please bring drinks

Location

Time

Call me if you have any questions.

Please RSVP either way.

See you there!

Looking forward to the fun we'll have.

Dear Wanda,

I recently read a book called THE PARTY. It's about throwing a singles party and having fun while finding true love. Who doesn't want that, right?

You're invited!

Please bring a guest of the opposite sex who would also like to meet someone special.

Guys — bring drinks

Girls — bring a dish

Time

Place

RSVP

Thanks. Looking forward to seeing you at The Party!

FOOD

Here's where you can have fun as well. What to bring? What to serve? Take a look at the menu below. I've asked two friends who are great cooks to contribute some easy and tasty recipes that are perfect for The Party.

Jessica, Gigi and I decided that the women would bring a dish of their choice and that the men would bring drinks. Of course, you can do this the other way around with men bringing the food and women the beverages. There was plenty of food and refreshments because basically everybody brought enough for a few people. The dining table was where we put the food. The drinks were on the counter in the kitchen. The co-hosts supplied the paper plates, cups, plastic forks, etc.

Another way to go is to hire a caterer and servers to set up before and clean up after. ThePartyTheBook.com website also offers different catering options.

MENU SUGGESTIONS FOR THE PARTY

Some party throwers love to cook and serve delicious food. For those of us who prefer other people's cooking, The Party Menu may take care of any pre-Party jitters.

I recommend being clear on the invitation. Women bring a dish. Men bring drinks. If you'd rather men participate more, have them bring a dish for four people. This can be as easy as a dip and a bag of chips or as elaborate as store-bought or home-cooked lasagna. A salad is pretty simple. So is picking up sandwiches from a deli and cutting them into quarters. Including vegetarian and vegan dishes is important these days. If you're a guest, bring what you like to eat.

Here are some special recipes if you'd like to have a few dishes there before The Party begins. Depending on the number of guests, you may want to double or triple the ingredients.

THAAO PENGHLIS
ACTOR/WRITER

My friend, Thaao, throws wonderful dinner parties. He's written two books about his remarkable travels, *Places*, and *Seducing Celebrities, One Meal at a Time*. And he's the writer and narrator on *Thaao Penghlis' The Lost Treasures Podcast*. He's a great cook. Here are a few of his recipes he shared with me for The Party.

Arugula and Watermelon Salad

Ingredients

◊   Arugula

◊   Fresh basil leaves

◊   3 plum tomatoes

◊   10 thin slices of watermelon

◊   5 ounces feta cheese, cubed

◊   Vinaigrette dressing

Directions

Toss everything together and serve.

MANGO/COCONUT CAKE

Ingredients

◊   2 cups all-purpose flour

◊   2 teaspoons baking soda

◊   1/2 teaspoon ground cloves

◊   1 teaspoon ground cinnamon

◊   1/2 cup unsweetened coconut

◊   1/2 teaspoon salt

◊   1 1/2 cups sugar

◊   4 eggs

◊   1/3 cup chopped walnuts

◊   1/3 cup chopped macadamia nuts

◊   1/4 cup vegetable oil

◊   2 cups ripe mango cut into small cubes

Cream

Ingredients

◊   1 cup heavy cream

◊   2 tablespoons sugar

◊   1 teaspoon vanilla

DIRECTIONS FOR THE CAKE

Pre-heat the oven to 350 degrees. Grease with butter a 9 x 6 loaf pan.
In a bowl, combine the flour, coconut, baking soda, cinnamon, cloves and

salt. In a separate bowl add the sugar, eggs, nuts and oil. Then add the mango and slowly fold the wet mixture into the flour mixture. Pour the ingredients into the greased pan and bake for 45 minutes. Check to see if it is fully baked by sticking a knife or toothpick in the center and seeing that it comes out clean.

DIRECTIONS FOR CREAM

Add sugar and vanilla to the cream and whip up until cream is stiff. Serve on top of sliced mango/coconut cake.

EFRAT CORNFELD
PERSONAL CHEF

Efrat enjoys a well-deserved busy career creating delicious recipes and cooking for international clients and private events.

SALMON TARTARE

Ingredients

◊   1/2 lb. salmon fillet cut into small cubes

◊   1 avocado cut into bigger cubes

◊   1 mango cut into bigger cubes

◊   1 teaspoon minced seeded jalapeño

◊   2 tablespoons minced red onion

◊   2 tablespoons cilantro minced

◊   1 teaspoon lemon zest and juice from 1 lemon

◊   1/2 teaspoon orange zest and juice from 1/2 an orange

◊   1/4 teaspoon lime zest and juice from 1 lime

◊   1 teaspoon Kosher or rock salt

◊   1/4 teaspoon pepper

◊   Thick potato chips, tortilla chips or thin crackers

DIRECTIONS

Mix all the above no longer than 1 hour before serving.
Place on potato chips.
Or serve in shot glasses with mini spoons.

Hummus Dip (Vegan option)

Ingredients

◊ 1 can chickpeas drained and rinsed with cool water

◊ 1/4 cup tahini paste

◊ 1 garlic clove

◊ 1 teaspoon cumin

◊ Juice from 1 lemon

◊ 1/2 teaspoon salt

◊ 2 tablespoons water

Directions

In food processor mix all ingredients for 5 minutes till smooth.
If you think it's a little thick, add water 1 teaspoon at a time.
Serve with crackers, pita chips, tortilla chips or as a veggie dip with cut up vegetables.

Beef Sliders

Ingredients

◊   1 lb. ground beef

◊   3 crushed garlic cloves

◊   1 1/2 teaspoons salt

◊   1/2 teaspoon black pepper

Directions

Heat oven to 425 degrees.
Mix all ingredients thoroughly.
Divide into 2 ounce chunks and form into little burgers.
Bake for 7-9 minutes.
Serve in slider buns with ketchup and a party pick.

RECIPES I'VE TRIED FOR THE PARTY

Fun Pizza Ties

Ingredients

◊   Store bought frozen pizza dough

◊   Olive oil

◊   Italian seasoning

◊   Grated Parmesan cheese

◊   Tomato sauce if desired

Directions

Pre heat oven – follow directions on the frozen dough container.
Thaw the pizza dough.
Sprinkle flour on a smooth cutting board.
Spread and roll out dough.
Sprinkle on olive oil and spread it with your fingers.
Sprinkle seasoning and cheese.
Cut dough into 1 inch strips.
Cut each strip into 5 inch lengths.
Gently tie the strips into a knot and tuck in the ends.
Place on oiled baking sheet and bake.
Serve alone or with a marinara dip.

Tuna and Cream Cheese Tortilla Pinwheels

Ingredients

◊ 1 package (8 ounces) cream cheese

◊ 1 can tuna, drained

◊ 1 cup shredded jack cheese

◊ 1 cup sour cream

◊ 1 can chopped green olives, drained

◊ 1 can chopped green chilies, drained

◊ 1/2 cup chopped green onions

◊ Garlic powder to taste

◊ Seasoned salt to taste

◊ 5 flour tortillas

◊ Salsa, optional

Directions

Beat cream cheese, cheese and sour cream until blended.
Add tuna and mix well.
Stir in olives, green chilies, green onions and seasonings.
Spread over tortillas; roll up tightly.
Wrap each in plastic wrap.
Refrigerate for several hours.
Unwrap and cut into ¾ inch slices, using a serrated knife.
Serve with salsa if desired.
Yield: about 4 dozen.

COCKTAILS

Cocktails can give The Party a certain flair. Here are three of my favorite recipes for pitchers. You can make the pitchers before the guests arrive. Just add soda water and ice right before serving.

Party Mojito Pitcher

Ingredients

◊   1/2 cup loosely packed mint leaves

◊   1/2 cup water

◊   1/2 cup sugar

◊   1 cup lime juice (8 limes)

◊   Extra lime cut into rounds

◊   2 cups white rum

◊   2 cups soda water or club soda

◊   1 sliced lemon

Directions

Add sugar, water and mint to a small saucepan. Heat over a medium flame. Bring to a simmer and stir until the sugar is dissolved. Turn off heat and allow to cool 5 minutes. Add to pitcher.
Add lime juice and rum to the pitcher.
Add extra mint leaves and slices of lime.
Fill pitcher with 4 handfuls of ice.
Add lemon slices from one lemon.
Gently stir in soda water before serving.

PINK SANGRIA WITH ROSÉ WINE PITCHER

Ingredients

- ◊   1 bottle of rosé
- ◊   1/2 cup vodka
- ◊   1/2 cup lemon juice
- ◊   2 tablespoons of granulated sugar
- ◊   1 cup sliced fresh strawberries
- ◊   1 cup fresh raspberries
- ◊   1 sliced orange
- ◊   1 sliced lemon
- ◊   2 tablespoons fresh mint
- ◊   2 cups soda, Sprite, club soda (whatever you prefer)

DIRECTIONS

Add all the fruit and mint to a large pitcher.
Add wine, vodka, lemon juice and sugar to the pitcher. Stir to combine.
Refrigerate for at least 2 hours and up to 24 hours before The Party.
Add soda immediately before serving.
Serve over ice and remember to ladle out the fruit into each glass.

Hawaiian Mimosa Pitcher

Ingredients

- ◊   1 cup coconut rum

- ◊   2 cups pineapple juice – cold

- ◊   1 bottle of Champagne or Prosecco

- ◊   Pineapple slices and cherries

DIRECTIONS

Combine all the liquid ingredients into a pitcher. Stir and serve over ice. Add pineapple slices and cherries for garnish.

DESSERTS

An endless choice, of course. Cookies are easy to buy or bake and so easy to serve.

Coffee and Tea are always a good idea if alcohol is being served.

DRINKS

Water

Wine – white and red

Beer

Sodas

♡

6. Okay, so you have guests arriving. Now what?

Good question. Here's where I did more brainstorming. Why were some social gatherings dull while others exciting? Why was it easy to meet someone at a certain event and totally impossible at another? What was the magic ingredient?

This is when the combo of Dr. Ruth and Oprah showed up in my mind. Both these popular relationship mentors advocate communication. Communication begins with Person A speaking to Person B. It continues with Person B responding to Person A. Then Person A says something else and voilà! A conversation.

But how do you go up to someone you don't know and talk to her or him? And how do you do this at a party where you may only know the host and the person you brought?

FIRST GAME

You know the game called Twenty Questions where you pretend to be a famous historical figure or celebrity or fictional character and someone has to guess who you are by asking questions that you can only answer "yes" or "no" to?

For example, I am Cleopatra. Someone asks if I'm alive. I answer, "No."

The next question could be, "Are you a woman?" I answer, "Yes." The next question could be, "Were you a real person?" I answer, "Yes." You have twenty questions to discover who I am.

This was the first game we played at The Party.

As soon as someone walked in, I quickly placed a nametag on his or her back. I said, "Welcome to The Party. You have twenty questions to find out who you are!" Naturally, they couldn't see what name was written on their nametag. So, they asked the other guests to look at their back and then proceeded to ask a question. This was instant communication. If they figured out who they were, they got to wear the name on their front. It's a lot of fun.

I remember at the second Party we threw, my friend, Leo, walked around with five nametags, like gold stars, on his chest. He got a lot of phone numbers that night.

WHAT HAPPENS NEXT?

What happens upon arrival and playing The Party Twenty Questions? Immediate interaction, laughter, fun, and playful guessing with strangers. Don't forget, everyone is in the exact same position so everyone will want to participate and get into the flow of The Party.

Have fun choosing names for The Party Twenty Questions because the more fun you, the host/hostess have, the more fun your guests will have. Nametags with a sticky back work best because they're made to stay on your clothes and peel off easily.

Find names inside and outside your world. You'll be surprised at how a conversation will start. At one Party, a guy guessed the name on the nametag was Picasso. What followed was an engaging conversation about art and Spain and then a plan to get together for some tapas the following week. Their second date turned out to be the beginning of a wonderful relationship.

A spark will ignite that will lead to heat…

Why is The Party Twenty Questions the first game?

It's the first game because it generates playfulness, conversation and interaction, which is exactly what's missing in most first encounters on dating apps and websites. They aren't fun because everyone is intimidated and it's hard to be yourself when you're "auditioning" for the part of someone's future boyfriend or girlfriend.

The Party's first game equalizes the guests. Let's all play. Let's all jump in. The water's fine.

THE PARTY TWENTY QUESTIONS

Here are some names for the nametags.

Marilyn Monroe	Abraham Lincoln	Mother Teresa
Kim Kardashian	John F. Kennedy	Martin Luther King
Winston Churchill	Bill Gates	Pink
Muhammad Ali	Mahatma Gandhi	Elvis Presley
Albert Einstein	Queen Elizabeth	Leonardo da Vinci
Pablo Picasso	Prince	Vincent Van Gogh
Hugh Jackman	Pope John Paul II	Rosa Parks
Thomas Edison	Ludwig Beethoven	Oprah Winfrey
Seth Rogen	Eva Peron	Dalai Lama
Neil Armstrong	Barack Obama	J.K. Rowling
Jesse Owens	Ernest Hemingway	David Bowie
Michael Jordon	Amy Schumer	Oscar Wilde
Coco Chanel	Pope Francis	Sting
Amelia Earhart	Alfred Hitchcock	Michael Jackson
Madonna	Cleopatra	Al Capone
Steve Jobs	Roger Federer	Sigmund Freud
Katherine Hepburn	Audrey Hepburn	David Beckham
Tiger Woods	King Charles III	Jackie Kennedy
Billie Holiday	J.R.R. Tolkien	Billie Jean King
Bugs Bunny	Homer Simpson	Rhaenyra Targaryen

Marge Simpson

Bilbo Baggins

Mickey Mouse

Fred Flintstone

Daffy Duck

Harry Potter

Tyrion Lannister

Beyoncé

James Bond

Babe Ruth

Scooby Doo

Minnie Mouse

Wilma Flintstone

Wonder Woman

Jon Snow

Meghan Markle

Harry Styles

Ben Stiller

Oprah Winfrey

Elton John

Charlie Brown

Eric Cartmen

Superman

Daenerys Targaryen

Taylor Swift

Jean-Michel Basquiat

Brad Pitt

♡

7. The Party continues...

Okay, so people have arrived, played The Party Twenty Questions game. Now what?

I went online and to a party store to find other ice-breaker games. I found Trivial Pursuit, Gender Bender, Cards Against Humanity, Charades and Pictionary. I also came up with thought provoking questions and wrote them on cards.

I suggest you stay away from board games like Monopoly because they're too myopic and exclusive when the purpose of a Party game is to meet new people. Ice-breaker games let guests flow in and out. They're about the people playing them and not about the game itself.

 I also arranged for a Salsa dance instructor to come and lead a dance class—but more about that later.

DESIGNATED AREAS

I assigned certain areas in my place to go with certain games. The front door opened into the living room, so that's where the first game, The Party Twenty Questions, took place.

In a corner of the living room I set up some chairs and a small table for

Gender Bender. It's a thought-provoking game where someone chooses a card, reads it and asks questions about how you would deal with the situation if you were the opposite sex. It makes you think, which is why I chose it. This game lends itself to people sharing ideas, opinions and stories.

Here's an example of how Gender Bender is played. A card says you work for a nasty boss who mistreats her staff on a daily basis. She berated you publicly about taking off too many sick days. It's time you asked for a raise. If you were a male, what would you do? If you were a female, what would you do? Does gender make a difference in this case?

What was revealing in this game was that sometimes we don't know what we think until we're asked a question specific to a certain subject. Not only did I discover what other people were thinking, I discovered what I was thinking. It was surprising and fun.

ACCEPTING YOURSELF

They say you can't be with someone until you can be with yourself. I know this is true for me. Why would you expect someone to enjoy your company if you don't enjoy your own company? We expect other people to fill our gaps for us. Instead, be curious about yourself. What interests you outside of what you have to do to simply live and make ends meet? Who's your favorite filmmaker? What's your favorite food? What countries do you want to visit? Do you enjoy concerts? What kind? Books? Politics? Sports? The more you participate in the world, the more interesting you'll become to yourself and to others.

If you're an introvert, then what books do you like? Do you meditate, draw, garden, solve crossword puzzles? And if so, would you like a companion who enjoys the same activities?

MORE, MUCH MORE…

The guests wandered over to the bar area and got a drink. I set up a small conversational area in the living room around the sofa that was cozy and comfortable. I made up a set of 4 x 5 Question Cards and put them on the coffee table. A guest would simply turn over a card and read the question out loud. A conversation would inevitably follow. Interesting answers and amusing stories were told. It was a way of getting to know a little more about someone in a casual, safe environment.

THE PARTY FUN QUESTIONS

- As a child, what did you wish to become when you grew up?

- If you were sent to live on a space station for three months and were only allowed to bring three personal items with you, what would they be?

- If you were stranded on a desert island, what three books would you want to have with you?

- What is one truth and one lie about your personality? Let the others guess which is which.

- What books or films have you read/seen recently that you would recommend?

- Would you rather be stranded on an island alone or with someone you dislike?

- You wouldn't be caught dead, where?

- What is the most bizarre encounter you have had in life (at work, personal, with friends or while travelling)?

- If you had a time machine that would work only once, what point in the future or the past would you visit?

- What crazy activities do you dream of trying someday?

- What is your idea of fun?

- What two things do you consider yourself to be very good at?

- What two things do you consider yourself to be very bad at?

- If money and time were no object, what would you be doing right now?

- What is something you hate doing?

- What is something you love doing?

- What is a hidden talent you have?

- Of all the places you have lived/visited, what was the one you like the best?

- What was the most meaningful compliment you have ever

received?

- Who was your childhood hero?
- What was your favorite music group in high school?
- Tell me the three best things about you.
- Which would you pick: being world-class attractive, a genius or famous for doing something great?
- Who are the three greatest living musicians in your opinion?
- What would you do if you were invisible for a day?
- Who would you like to live like for a day?
- If you could live in any TV home, what would it be?
- If you could eat only three foods for the rest of your life, what would they be?
- What's your favorite childhood book?
- If you could ask your pet three questions, what would they be?
- What's the most courageous thing you've ever done?
- Who would play you in a movie of your life?
- If you could be an Olympic athlete, in what sport would you compete?
- If you could choose your own nickname, what would it be?
- Who is the funniest person you know?
- What do you think is the greatest invention of all time?
- Would you rather win an Olympic medal, an Academy Award or the Nobel Peace prize?
- What's your favorite time of day?
- What's your favorite season?
- If you could ask the President one question, what would it be?
- What's your dream job?
- What is the scariest movie you've ever seen?
- If you could travel anywhere in the world, where would it be?

- What is your favorite family tradition?

- Who's your celebrity crush?

- What are you good at?

- Would you rather spend five days exploring Yosemite, Disneyland or New York City?

- What personal trait has gotten you in the most trouble?

- Which celebrity chef would you most like to fix you a meal?

- What is the best piece of advice you've received?

- If you had to pick a new name for yourself, what name would you pick?

- Would you rather be the most popular kid in school or the smartest kid in school?

- What do you like to do on a rainy day?

- Would you rather be the best player on a horrible team or the worst player on a great team?

- Which of the Seven Dwarfs is most like you?

- If someone made a movie of your life would it be a drama, a comedy, a romantic-comedy, action film, or science fiction?

- If you were guaranteed to be successful in a different profession, what would you want to do?

8. What you'll discover

I love going to see plays. I always have and I always will. I remember being twelve years old and going to a matinee all by myself at the Royal Alex Theatre in downtown Toronto. The play was "Abelard and Heloise," a tragic love story between a nun and a priest (what were they thinking?). I sat in the cheap seats and cried at the end when they couldn't be together. It's still one of the best theatrical experiences of my life because that production did what art is supposed to do—transport you and emotionally move you in a way that changes you forever.

Have I dated men who don't care for the theatre? Yes. Did I marry one? Yes. But he's now my ex. This isn't the reason we're no longer together, but it's interesting that my present husband loves seeing plays. We've had great experiences going to the theatre and we've even created theatre together.

But back to those single years. When I was between husbands, I met a very attractive man at one of my Parties. Ted was a doctor. I had two things in common with him - I had played a doctor on TV, and we were both smitten with him. He drove a silver Porsche, he had more suits than the Men's Department at Bloomingdale's and he had several ex-wives. Still, I really liked him. That is, until we went to see a play at the Mark Taper Forum in downtown LA. The play was gripping—a Jean

Claude van Itallie production of "The Traveler." I was totally mesmerized. I looked over at Ted, expecting to see a man totally absorbed in the play. Instead, I saw a man totally asleep. Strike one!

He had a lot of guilty baggage due to his behaving badly with his exes. And, he was very willing to dump it all on me. After a few months, I was exhausted from carrying around his past on my shoulders. Strike two! And, well, the sex wasn't great. Like I said, he was smitten with himself, so in bed it was all about him and very little about me. Strike three! And he's out!

My point? Don't settle. Look for someone who likes to do some of the things you like to do. Perhaps he won't go to a dance concert with you, (my husband isn't a dance fan), so I go with a friend. But, as mentioned before, we both love the theatre. We make trips to London and New York for the plays. We also produce plays that he writes and I direct. Theatre unifies us. For some couples it's golf or hiking. We have friends who play musical instruments. After dinner, she sits at the piano and he takes out his guitar. Playing music brings them together.

Participating in the different games at The Party lends itself to the discovery of compatibility. Watch and listen and you'll find out if he likes to do the things you like to do: travel, watch films, cook, ride horses, skydive, watch or play soccer or golf, go to museums, plays, concerts, play chess, snorkel, etc. At The Party, you'll observe who has an affinity for the things you like. You don't need to share your every interest, but it's definitely a big advantage to have at least a few significant interests in common.

YOU SAY YOU'RE NOT A GAMES PERSON

That's fine. Wander into the area that's designated for just sitting, relaxing and easy communicating. Conversation is the foundation of The Party. Too often, you don't have the opportunity to be yourself at parties because you're spending all your energy shouting to be heard. You'll observe that during The Party, pretty much everyone will gravitate to this quiet area from time to time. If you have a backyard, create a place that has soft lights, a few chairs, and a couple of small tables, and you'll be all set. A quiet area in the living room or den are other places you could designate as a conversation corner.

HOW TO START A CONVERSATION

First of all, remember that everyone is in the same boat as you are. We're all human beings, trying our best. Some of us are shy, some aren't. Here are a few conversation openers. For fun ice-breaker questions, check out the list in Chapter 7 (page 53).

Smile. A smile looks good on everyone. It inspires confidence—your own and the other person's. You're more approachable and attractive when you smile. A smile is healthy. It signals the brain to produce endorphins which cause reduced levels of stress, and serotonin which creates feelings of happiness and well-being.

Find something about the other person that you like. Perhaps you overheard them talking about sailing and you love sailing. Let them know. Maybe he's wearing a jacket and you like the color. Tell him. Let's say you've just seen a film you love, ask if she's seen it. If she hasn't, then ask what kind of films she likes. Every sentence is a springboard to another sentence or question and voilà, you're exchanging ideas, opinions, and feelings. In other words, you are having a conversation.

Try not to be self-conscious. I know this is like saying don't think about the pink elephant, but it's important. Focus on the other person and not on yourself. Be genuinely interested in the person you're talking to.

Really listen. If all he's doing is talking about himself, move on. But if he asks you about your interests, your experiences, your opinions, then stay a bit longer. Smile and answer. Then see if he's a good listener.

MORE FUN POSSIBILITIES

Here's another thing I did that I encourage you to do when planning The Party. Think about something outside of the box you would enjoy experiencing at The Party. Imagine yourself as a guest. What unique activity would you like to participate in?

This was easy for me. As I mentioned, I love dancing. I go to dance concerts. I love moving to music. The simplest way I describe how dance affects me is that it makes me happy. So, I decided to hire a Salsa dance instructor for The Party to lead a beginner's class for anyone who was interested.

I contacted a few dance schools and found a Salsa instructor. I hired her for a couple of hours. The backyard patio became the dance floor. She arrived at 9:00 and led a very easy, playful class for forty-five minutes. She brought her own music and speakers. Twelve people joined in, and an affinity group of Salsa lovers was created at The Party. The dancers had such a great time that they exchanged numbers and organized an outing for the following weekend at a dance club in Santa Monica. It was that group's "second date" - easy, no pressure - just a whole lot of Salsa fun.

Take a few minutes and think about what you and your co-hosts really enjoy. Here's my list. Have fun making your own.

INTERESTS

Horror films – set up a room where you play several horror films throughout the evening. You'll definitely connect with other horror fans.

Sports – Put out sports magazines on a coffee table with some questions you come up with about certain teams and statistics. You'll attract guests who also love sports to that corner of the room.

Cooking – Put out food magazines and special desserts in small spoon-size bites. Have pencils nearby with a questionnaire so the guests can guess what the ingredients are. Conversations about favorite restaurants, chefs, TV food shows will follow.

Politics – Designate a corner where hot topics of the day are discussed. I recommend a 2-minute timer on the table to limit the opinions expressed. Remember, the idea of these affinity corners is to attract people with similar interests. Keep it light and fun if you can. Good luck with that in the politics corner!

Art – Place several art books on a table with pages open to provocative pieces. The idea is to create an atmosphere of curiosity and fun. Have information about an art exhibit in town and a signup sheet for guests who'd like to go on their "second date."

Travel – Easy. Put a globe on a coffee table along with an atlas and some travel magazines and some questions like:

- What's the best place you've ever been to?
- The worst?
- What are your bucket list destinations?
- If you could be stranded anywhere, where would you choose?
- Where was the scariest place you've ever traveled?
- The place where you had the most fun?
- Least fun?
- Sexiest fun?

♡

9. Fate or destiny

When I was in my mid 30s, I was visiting my parents in Toronto, the city where I was born. When my parents immigrated to Canada they were very poor, and my mother was seven months pregnant with me when they arrived.

The first winter was terribly cold. Our neighbor was an older woman named Mrs. Feldman. She kindly offered my mother the snowsuit of her then 2-year-old grandson who had outgrown it. My mother was very appreciative and I wore that snowsuit until I outgrew it myself.

I had heard this story about Mrs. Feldman and my wearing her grandson's snowsuit many times over the years. That afternoon, as I was lying on the floor doing some yoga stretches, my mother mentioned it again. Here I was, newly divorced and trying to figure out my life. I'd made the trip home to get the kind of love only family and old friends can provide.

My mother said, "Isn't it funny that Mrs. Feldman was Adam's grandmother?"

"Adam who?" I asked.

"Adam Diamond, your boyfriend when you were 16 years old," she answered.

"Adam Diamond!" I sat up. "My first love?"

My mother nodded.

"You mean to tell me that all this time I didn't realize that the woman in the story, Mrs. Feldman, who gave me the snowsuit, was Adam's grandmother?" I couldn't believe it. Then it hit me. "Wait a minute! What you're telling me is that when I was 1 year old, I wore a little boy's snowsuit—the same boy I didn't actually meet until fifteen years later when I was 16 and he was 17?" My head was spinning. "And that little boy turned out to be my first true love, Adam Diamond? Is that what you're telling me?"

"Yes," she said. "You should listen better."

I was so shocked that I almost couldn't grasp what I'd just figured out. Adam and I fell in love in high school, and after a beautiful, sweet, sexy, teenage relationship of over a year, he decided he wanted to meet other girls and broke up with me. I was 17 and totally devastated. He moved to a different high school, and I never saw him again. I heard he ended up marrying his next girlfriend (ironic, wouldn't you say?) and went to law school.

The last time I was in Toronto, I thought I'd look him up. There he was on my screen, just the same but older. His photo made me smile though I felt uncertain about calling him. What would I say? "Hi, Adam, it's me, Terri. Remember? I was your first. You were mine. Oh, and there's a story about a snowsuit you won't believe…"

I did call him. We met for a drink at 4 PM that lasted until 8 PM. We reminisced and laughed a lot. He actually apologized for the way he ended things. I forgave him. He told me he tried to get in touch over the years, but for some reason I never got the messages. We hugged goodbye and I felt complete.

Do you believe in fate? What about destiny? Aren't they the same? No, not really. They're used interchangeably in today's vernacular but there is a difference in their meanings.

Fate is believed to be inevitable and unchangeable whereas an individual can change their destiny.

Is it fate that you throw The Party and meet your true love? Or is it destiny?

My story about Adam and the snowsuit is a perfect example of fate. It was inevitable for us to meet again because I believe it was a pre-ordained and beyond our control kind of love.

A similar but different experience happened with the man who would become my first husband.

I was living in Los Angeles. It was my first year here and I was trying to figure out how to survive as an actress. I was working as a waitress and going to acting class. Through a friend at the gym, I met a guy named Weston who worked in publicity for A&M Records. He asked me out to a concert for a band his company represented called Super Tramp. After the show, we went to a party for the band at a hotel—pretty girls and cool guys—a typical Hollywood party.

A year later, I was working as a hostess at a restaurant in Hollywood on Highland Avenue called Hampton's. It was a trendy, upscale hamburger joint with a big tree in the patio that had a sign that read "No autographs, please."

One day, a group of six people—three guys, three girls—came in. I showed them to their table. When they were leaving, one of the men came up to me and asked, "See the guy who just left?"

"Yes," I said. The guy was tall and handsome with bright blue eyes who smiled at me when I showed them to their table.

"Well," he said, "that guy is in love with you."

"Really?" I grinned. "Then he should tell me that."

The next day, at lunch, in walked the tall, handsome, blue-eyed guy.

"Table for one?" I asked.

"No," he answered. "I was wondering if you're free to go out with me."

"Yes," I said. "I am."

"Okay, great, how about this Friday night?"

And that was the beginning of a one-year courtship that led to a ten-year marriage.

One day, early on in the courtship—maybe two weeks in—we were talking about music. Emanuel was a photographer who worked for A&M Records. I told him I'd seen Super Tramp and had been at the after-party. He went over to his file cabinet, and a few minutes later, came back with several proof sheets.

"Take a look," he smiled.

I soon realized these were proof sheets from that same Super Tramp after-party. He was the A&M photographer for the event.

Now, you're probably thinking, okay, that's kind of cool, both of us being at the same party the year before. But it went beyond that. As I continued to look at the proofs, I saw pictures of myself that Emanuel had taken. There were at least 10 shots of me looking directly into the camera! I didn't remember him taking these pictures, but there they were, portrait after portrait of me smiling at the camera—at the photographer—at my future husband. And these were pictures taken at a party we both attended one year before we actually met at the restaurant. Now, is this another sign of fate? I think so because our being together created our beautiful son.

When I think about these two similar events, I'm struck that twice in my life I "met" my future partner long before I actually met him.

Here's another true story. My neighbor, Ryan, was driving on Olympic Boulevard going west. He stopped at a red light. A car in the next lane also stopped. Sitting in the passenger seat was an extremely pretty woman. She looked over at Ryan and they smiled at each other. He was newly divorced, feeling quite lousy about life, but for some reason, he had the courage to roll down his window and talk to her. She motioned that her window was broken, so she opened her car door.

Ryan quickly gave her his card and said, "Please call me." The light turned green and they both went in different directions. She went straight and he turned right.

She never called.

A few months later, Ryan decided to get serious about finding a new relationship and contacted a matchmaker. He paid the fee, filled out the forms and waited. The matchmaker called three weeks later and said she had the perfect candidate for him who happened to be a close friend.

Ryan said, "Sure, please tell her about me."

A week later, a woman called.

She said, "You won't believe this, but I have your card in my wallet. When the matchmaker told me your name, I knew it sounded familiar and I looked at the card and it was you!"

Yes, the woman Ryan gave his card to at the stoplight was the same woman the matchmaker recommended. Ryan was overjoyed. He thought this must be fate. They went out on a date – breakfast at the Beverly Hilton Hotel.

But that was pretty much it. The matchmaker told Ryan that the woman, Amanda, wasn't quite ready to say goodbye to her ex-boyfriend.

The ending of this story isn't what you expected. You wanted Ryan and Amanda to end up together, but that wasn't how it played out. What it did do for Ryan was open his mind and heart again to the possibility of meeting someone, which is a pretty powerful thing in itself.

I'm married to a wonderful man. When we talk about the places we used to frequent before we met—the Hollywood YMCA, Runyan Canyon, Santa Monica beach—and the friends we learnt we had in common—Janie, Caleb and Kendra—we suspect that our paths would have eventually crossed.

Why am I bringing fate and destiny up when writing about The Party? Because it's a new and untried avenue for meeting friends who can connect you to more potential friends. And who knows, maybe you'll meet someone you've met before and fate will play out its hand. Or maybe you'll have a say in changing your path and creating your own destiny.

Paths cross and then cross again. Life is unpredictable. Sometimes predetermined fate is carving out the steps you take. Sometimes, that elusive reality you have a hand in creating, destiny, is providing the opportunity for you to make your dreams come true.

Either way, take a chance on The Party! What I know for sure is staying at home in front of the TV will keep you staying at home in front of the TV. And you never know, you may actually have some fun!

I've always been inspired by the following Chinese proverb:

*If you don't change your direction,
you'll end up where you're headed.*

♡

10. How do you meet people?

In the past, marriages were arranged, and in some cultures, they still are. Today, you usually meet someone when a friend or family member sets you up on a blind date, or you go to a bar or, more commonly, on the Internet.

People did and do actually connect through these events and platforms. True love is possible even in the weirdest of times because true love does exist. Even if you don't believe it, true love believes it. Because it is a force of its own.

It was fate that I met the partners I have met. I think this is true not only for the loves of my life, but for everyone I've met and have a connection with.

There is a saying—People come into your life for a reason, a season or a lifetime. I've thought about this quite a bit. Usually, I can determine if a particular friendship was for a reason, a season or a lifetime. But there was one situation where I couldn't figure out why on earth I flew up to Northern California to have a weekend with a certain man.

Soon after my divorce, I got a call from my TV commercial agent, Denise, saying that someone called her and wanted to talk to me because we had the same unusual last name. I said, sure, why not. I'd never heard of him.

Maybe he was a distant relative of my ex-husband's since I'd kept his name. So, I gave her permission to give him my number.

A few days later, he called and told me he'd been at a race where someone had asked if he knew me. He was interested in finding out who had the same last name so he tracked me down. He also heard I was an actress and that had piqued his interest as well.

He had such a kind voice and gentlemanly way about him. We talked several times, and we decided to meet. He was a racecar driver after having been one of the most successful hydroplane racers in the world. He was prepping for a race so I flew up for the weekend.

Being at Laguna Seca raceway was like entering another galaxy. He took me around the racetrack in his sports car. I was never so scared and thrilled in my life. Later, we had a fun dinner and talked for several hours.

I brought up two very different types of "teddies." One was a very sexy, black, lace teddy and the other was my little teddy bear I slept with after my first husband and I split up. My friend, Chanise, thought it was a good idea to bring both, just in case.

He turned out to be a true gentleman. We slept in our own rooms. I must admit I was a little disappointed. But I knew it was the right thing to do.

I flew home the next day. He called several times after that, but it was clear to us both that a long-distance relationship wasn't ideal. The amusing coincidence of having the same last name wasn't a good enough reason to start a relationship.

For a while, I couldn't figure out why I flew up there. Why would I ever want to get involved with a racecar driver? He'd already been injured many times while racing his hydroplanes; it was just a matter of time. So, I was left with a feeling of confusion and discomfort whenever I thought about that weekend. What was our "reason"? It certainly didn't turn out to be a season or a lifetime. It was a few turns around a racetrack.

I just Googled him. He eventually retired from racing. He did a web series about boats. He volunteers with several charities. He still seems like a great person.

While writing this, I realize I flew up there because I was willing to take a chance, and so was he. And what's not great about that? That was the "reason" for our relationship—taking a chance, going for the gold, believing in yourself, creating the possibility of good things happening in your life.

And, who knows, maybe one day when I'm in Seattle, we'll have coffee.

$\heartsuit$

11. More musings

Social media was created to connect people, but in reality, it separates them.

I read a study that reported that people feel worse after they've been on social media than before. Like it or not, we humans compare ourselves to one another. We count our "likes" and compete with our friends' "likes." We hold back liking someone for countless negative reasons. Yep, just like high school. For most people, high school was a tough time filled with emotional highs and lows. So why would anyone want to go through those times again? Maybe our curiosity about others is too great to keep us away from things that aren't really healthy.

It's so easy for social media to take over. I speak from experience. I've deleted a lot of apps and now spend very little time searching the web, unless, of course, it's for great shoes. That, I may never give up.

DATING? DO PEOPLE STILL DATE?

I asked friends to share their Internet dating stories. Some were funny, some weird, some awful, and only two led to good relationships. The anxiety levels were always high, they said. The meetings were awkward and the actual dating was mostly disappointing.

Anna, 23 years old, said she'd rather stay home with her two cats, her Sam Heughan poster, a glass of red wine and watch old movies than risk meeting the next Jeffrey Dahmer.

Jack, 37 years old, did meet his true love. It was his 1st date on the site. It was her 42nd.

Bianca is a lovely woman in her 60s. She met a man on a website who said he was late 60s, athletic, tall, retired and divorced. They made plans to meet at a restaurant. When Bianca walked in, she saw a man in his 80s, stooped over, trying to read the menu. She assumed he wasn't her date. She was wrong.

Melissa liked guys a few years younger than herself. She was in her late 40s. She was honest about her age and was delighted when she found men on a site that preferred older women. She had a date with John, 42, that she thought went well.

Afterward, he texted her and said, "I thought you'd be younger."

She texted him back, "I thought you'd be smarter."

Lucy, 34, decided to go on a dating website because she wasn't meeting anyone. She posted that she didn't need someone to make her happy because she already was. She wanted to meet someone who would add to her life.

Bennet responded, "I'm intrigued." They met at a Mexican restaurant, married a couple of years later and are still together.

William was 68 and had recently lost his wife of 35 years. He decided to go on a singles cruise to the Bahamas. There were so many available women on the ship that he felt totally overwhelmed. He also felt uncomfortable when within the first five minutes of conversation, his dining companions would ask how much money he had and if he was leaving everything to his grown children.

I was having coffee with a girlfriend at a neighborhood Peet's Coffee Shop. We were sitting outside. I noticed a man at a nearby table with an attractive woman. I glanced up a few minutes later. He was still there but the woman sitting opposite him was a different one. He was there for several hours. Every thirty minutes a new woman sat down to meet him. He was serial coffee dating. It was like he was auditioning them to be his girlfriend. Actually, he was.

Kate, 41, met a man on a sailboat party who was overweight and slightly obnoxious. He told her he was dating four different women—a dentist, a lawyer, a teacher and a city planner.

How, she thought, was this guy possibly dating four interesting, attractive women? He told Kate he was on a dating site called J Date. So, she went on the site thinking that if he could date great women, she could date great men.

She met five men. Man Number Three turned out to be a good match. They dated and a year later, married. During their marriage, Kate became quite friendly with her new sister-in-law, Patty. Kate and Man Number Three divorced six years later. Two years after that, her now ex-sister-in-law, Patty, called and said she had a friend she wanted her to meet. That friend, Trenton, became Kate's present and (she hopes) forever husband.

So, if it weren't for Mr. Obnoxious on the boat, Kate would never have met her true love, Trenton.

Jodi, 32, was on Match.com. She liked a picture of a man who looked athletic and handsome. He liked her, too, so they decided to meet for a drink. She was very happy to see that he looked like his photo. They had a drink. She noticed he was talking quickly and never looked directly at her.

He said, "Let's go back to my place."

She said, "I think you're high."

He said, "I am."

She said, "Bye."

A funny story. I was having dinner in Hollywood with my friend, Rachel. She was in her 40s and starting to get back into dating. She'd had three unsuccessful marriages and had taken a long break from relationships. During dinner, she told me that several years before she had had breast implants. She was feeling insecure about them now that she was ready to venture back into the dating scene.

She asked, "Can I show them to you and you'll tell me if they look okay?"

"Sure," I shrugged.

We went to the bathroom and entered a stall together. She lifted her sweater and undid her bra.

"They look fine to me," I said.

"But how do they feel? I don't want anyone to touch them and think they aren't real. Can you feel them, please, and let me know?"

"Okay," I answered. I was a good friend.

I felt them and said, "They feel fine to me but I've never touched a pair of breasts except for my own. I should have experimented in college." So, I felt my breast to compare and said, "Yep, they feel pretty much like mine. I think you're good to go."

A woman walked into the bathroom. Rachel and I looked at each other and burst out laughing. What could we possibly do but walk out of the cubicle together, wash our hands and go back to our dinners? Which is exactly what we did. A hilarious moment, but the message is clear that returning to the dating scene draws our insecurities to the surface. The Party provides the opportunity to overcome them in a safe and playful environment.

Eva was 62 and a widow. She'd been married most of her life so when Lawrence died, she felt isolated and lonely. Her sister suggested she go on a dating website. Her first date was with a younger man from Australia. In spite of her family's objections, they married within months. As soon as he got his green card, he filed for divorce.

Elise, 36, met a man on Bumble. They went out for dinner. He spent the whole time talking about his ex-wife, Marsha. (That seems to happen a lot). He walked Elise to her car and they had a rather long, hot kiss. Elise was now interested.

Then he said, "If only I'd kissed Marsha like that."

I'm not suggesting you give up on Tinder or Bumble or Match.com, etc. I know people who've met some interesting men and women this way. Read the reviews. I recently did and the number of users who felt ripped off by the apps didn't surprise me. The reviewers were also clear about wanting an app where you could meet a possible mate rather than meet a possible hook up.

The Party offers a whole new way of meeting people you would probably never meet otherwise. And remember, the second idea of The Link Effect is to only invite people who sincerely want to find true love.

I recall the moment I spoke those words out loud. A friend asked me what I wanted.

"True love," I answered. "That's what I want. Yes, that's what I'm looking for."

It was an epiphany. I realized I'd been ashamed to admit it to myself or to anyone else. So when I said the words out loud, "True love," I felt totally authentic. It was a beautiful moment. Being honest like that changed the way I thought about my life and the partner I wanted. It opened my heart.

Try saying it out loud now to yourself. "I want true love." Let yourself breathe in those words. Inhale deeply. Do it a couple of times. Then let yourself smile. Feels good, doesn't it?

♡

12. Treat yourself well

I like therapy. I think it should be part of one's health regime. The mind needs care just like the body. Having a safe place and person to go to is one of the paths to a well-balanced life. A friend or family member isn't equipped to handle intimate details you may want to share. They could feel compromised in some way. Speaking with a professional therapist frees you up to say what you need to say which enables you to work on your challenges together. You can walk out of the office without any concerns about the thoughts and secrets you just shared. Therapists are your allies. They are unbiased. You pay them for a service.

I see a therapist, Sarah, who is smart, insightful and caring. Her main goal is to help me become the best, happiest, most productive me I can be. We've gone through many dark moments of my life together. With her help, I've grown and come out on the other side—stronger and more appreciative of myself and other people.

I also look for great coaches, teachers and mentors. I actively seek these people out. They've taught me more about life and myself than I could've learned on my own. They offer support and perspective. Some of these mentors I've never actually met. I've read their books or listened to them speak. Others, I've sought out because there are only so many true spiritual leaders and gurus alive right now in the world. If I have the opportunity to see the Dalai Lama or the hugging saint, Amma, I take that opportunity. Or if there's a well-respected acting coach like Larry Moss teaching, I'll try to attend his class. Now, with TED talks and YouTube, you can track speakers, alive or dead, like Dr. Brené Brown, Louise Hay, Wayne Dyer, Eckart Tolle, Deepak Chopra, Phil Stutz, Alan Watts - people who have dedicated their lives to helping others reach their highest potential.

Here are some thoughts and sayings about love and life that have stayed with me over the years. My office walls are covered with these reminders of love, laughter, beauty, success and all things positive.

Don't believe everything you think.

–Allan Lokos

I fell in love the way you fall asleep: slowly, and then all at once.

–John Green

Unable to perceive the shape of you, I find you all around me. Your presence fills my eyes with your love; it humbles my heart, for you are everywhere.

–unknown Poet
The Shape of Water

I'm selfish, impatient and a little insecure. I've made mistakes, I am out of control and at times hard to handle. But if you can't handle me at my worst, then you sure as hell don't deserve me at my best.

–Marilyn Monroe

I love you without knowing how, or when, or from where. I love you simply, without problems or pride: I love you in this way because I do not know any other way of loving but this, in which there is no I or you, so intimate that your hand upon my chest is my hand, so intimate that when I fall asleep your eyes close.

–Pablo Neruda

You don't love someone because they're perfect, you love them in spite of the fact that they're not.

–Jodi Picoult

If you can't dance, what's the point of a revolution?

–Emma Goldman

We do not see things the way they are. We see them as we are.

–Talmud

Life shrinks or expands in proportion to one's courage.

–Anais Nin

Let there be spaces in your togetherness, and let the winds of the heavens dance between you. Love one another but make not a bond of love: Let it be rather a moving sea between the shores of your souls.

–Khalil Gibran
The Prophet

Once upon a time there was a boy who loved a girl, and her laughter was a question he wanted to spend his whole life answering.

–Nicole Krauss
The History of Love

Never love anyone who treats you like you're ordinary.

–Oscar Wilde

Any man who can drive safely while kissing a pretty girl is simply not giving the kiss the attention it deserves.

–Albert Einstein

Being someone's first love may be great, but to be his or her last love is beyond perfect.

–Anonymous

Every love story is beautiful, but ours is my favorite.

–Anonymous

If I get married, I want to be very married.

–Audrey Hepburn

After a while, you just want to be with the one who makes you laugh.

–Mr. Big to Carrie
from Sex and the City

♡

13. Comfort chemistry

Sexual chemistry is when the touch, smell, taste, sound and sight of another person stirs you up in those very same senses. When all those senses are stimulated, you want to become involved sexually with that person. I hope you've felt that.

I believe there is another phenomenon called Comfort Chemistry. That's when you can just be yourself with the other person. "Be" is such a small word but it means so much. It means the freedom to exist exactly the way you are. It means ease and no pressure. You feel no fear of losing something or someone because of who you are. It means love. Comfort Chemistry includes a balance of your higher and more evolved self with your other self that isn't as elevated but still a part of you. It means two energies coming together in a calm and playful way.

The ability for two or more people to just hang out and enjoy one another and themselves is the beauty of Comfort Chemistry. No inner negative mind-chatter. No "Devil" and "Angel" on your shoulders tempting you. It's a deep, life-affirming breath of fresh air. It's the smile on your face that's there just because the person you're with is exactly who he is at that moment. You know the statement, "It's so easy being with him"? That's Comfort Chemistry.

What became clear from these Parties, is that people gravitated towards people they were comfortable with as well as attracted to. Attraction is number one, of course—that unknown, unconscious pull that connects two people. But let's not underestimate comfort. If a person makes you feel jittery and nervous, it may be "love." Or it may be your intuition telling you this person isn't good for you. If you can't be yourself when you're around him or her, then maybe you shouldn't be considering this person for a relationship. That individual may not be the loving, nurturing and supportive partner you want in your life.

My friend, Jasmine, 29, had a boyfriend she met online named Frank. She was crazy about him. She was so excited to see him that she barely slept the night before or ate the day of their date. This went on for six months. Her "butterflies" soon became a nervous stomach. She started taking anti-acid medication, which didn't help. Only when Frank left town for work did her stomach feel better. When she finally broke up with him, she found out he'd been cheating on her from day one. He finally confessed to being incapable of committing to a monogamous relationship. As soon as she told him to leave, her health improved. They had the opposite of Comfort Chemistry. They had Discomfort Chemistry—a term I just coined.

The Party can help you answer important questions. You'll know if there's Comfort Chemistry with someone you meet because you'll be able to talk, dance and relax with him or her in several areas of the venue. You'll also see how that person is with other people.

You'll register how you feel when you're near him. Let your body tell you if you're yourself when this person is close by. Let your heart tell you if it feels warm and strong. Be curious. Stay present. Be comfortable in your confidence. Breathe. Observe. Then ask yourself if you'd like to spend more time with him. Does he or she make you feel good? Is she kind? Is he funny? You'll be surprised to see how simply and quickly the answers come.

As hosts of The Party, you have the responsibility of making sure it's going well. I found being a co-hostess a great job. I met everybody. I got to interact with different groups. I made sure the food and drinks were available. I joined in on conversations and then moved on to other games and conversations. I was a free agent. And yes, I met someone at the first Party we threw. His name was Liam. He was divorced. He was a lawyer who secretly wanted to be an actor. (I find that most lawyers secretly want to be actors). We went out for drinks a week later and started a sweet romance. About four months into our relationship, he asked me out for an early dinner. I assumed we would spend the evening and night together. But at 8:30 PM, he said he had to go.

"Where?" I asked. "It's Saturday night and we're on a date."

He told me his therapist said he shouldn't jump back into a monogamous relationship so soon after his divorce. He had another date lined up that evening.

I said, "Great that you're in therapy, but I'm interested in having a monogamous relationship, so let's say goodbye now."

He cried. Yes, he did. He asked me to be patient and understanding.

A few weeks later I told my friend, Liz, about the breakup. I was still disturbed that Liam had cried. Maybe he really did have strong feelings for me?

Liz said, "He's a crier. That's what he does. Forget him!"

So, I threw another Party!

♡

14. What to wear to The Party

I don't know about you, but I love to get dressed up. It must be my acting background. When I'd get an audition, I'd go directly to my closet to figure out what the character would wear (that I happened to have in my closet).

I'm not a slave to fashion, though. I prefer clothes that are interesting and express the different sides of who I am.

When I was taking pictures of actors—my other career was a headshot photographer—I would go over their wardrobe and help them decide what to bring to the photo session. When I had a female client, I started the wardrobe conversation by saying she should wear whatever made her feel terrific. And I also told her to wear really great underwear.

"Why? We aren't doing those kinds of pictures, are we?"

"No," I said. "I think how you feel about yourself starts with your underwear. It can be a source of your feminine power." The actress took my advice and showed up feeling confident and strong, which came through in her pictures.

I suggest you start with your underwear when it comes to the question of "What do I wear?" No one but you will see your underwear. Even if you meet someone who is amazing, it's better that he doesn't see you in your bra and panties until the time is right! More about that later…

When I knew I was going to be intimate with the man I was seeing, I went to a lingerie shop on Montana Boulevard in Santa Monica. I told the saleswoman that tonight was going to be "the night." It had been a while since I'd slept with someone so I was more than a little nervous. I asked her to put together a sexy outfit for me.

"What makes you feel sexy?" she asked.

"Me? But shouldn't I dress for him?"

"No," she shook her head. "Dress for yourself. Always. What makes you feel sexy will definitely make him feel sexy. Trust me."

I did. The outfit was a success.

Once you've decided on the underwear, go to your closet and use the de-clutter guru, Marie Kondo's, simple and brilliant tip. "What sparks joy?" That blue, suede skirt you bought on a whim in San Francisco? That great pair of black jeans you got at the AG outlet outside of Las Vegas? That beautiful, silver sequin dress you got in Paris? That casual white T-shirt, blue jeans and red ankle-high boots you got in Toronto? Wear whatever sparks your joy so that when you look in the mirror, you smile and say, "Yes! That's me!"

And if nothing sparks your joy, then go shopping with a friend who has a great sense of style.

There was an experiment I read about in a fashion magazine. Five women were each given $750 to buy clothes. Then they were given another $750 to buy clothes but this time they had to go with a good friend and buy what their friend suggested.

In every case, the outfits bought with the friend were more flattering and cooler than the clothes bought on her own. The magazine printed photos of both sets of clothes. The women's second wardrobe was more exciting and appealing than the first.

I recently met a CEO of a marketing firm, Millie, 45, who told me she had tons of clothes but felt she never had anything to wear. She longed to have a unique style that represented her as the powerful and successful woman she was. I took her shopping. I suggested she try on a smartly tailored red silk dress. Red was a color she stayed away from. I added a simple black leather blazer and knee-high boots. She finally looked as dynamic on the outside as she felt on the inside.

Sometimes we need a little help from our friends. New doors will open. I promise.

The past ten plus years, I've had the good fortune of working with a stylist/designer named Biannti. She has a studio in Sherman Oaks where she has seasonal shopping shows and helps design and build her clients' wardrobes. She also has her own line of simple and elegant tops and skirts called BIA MIRO.

She is a genius when it comes to color and style. She's very up front and will tell you in an instant to take something off if it doesn't do anything for you. I have clothes in my closet that are unique, special and suited for me. This goes from casual jeans to special event outfits.

Here are some of Biannti's thoughts on dressing for The Party:

"Like it or not, clothes are the first thing anyone sees. They tell the story of who you are. Are you worthy of their interest? There isn't anything more important for a first meeting than what you wear!"

ADVICE FOR WOMEN

"If you're looking for true love, the most important advice I can give is dress more covered than bare. There are so many things you can wear now to display a lovely figure or to disguise figure flaws in a tasteful way.

Plunging necklines or ridiculously short skirts are strictly taboo. The old school catch phrase about leaving something to the imagination holds true today. More cover is a sure sign of confidence, which is very attractive.

The other piece of advice is to go with color. Years of working with men on dressing themselves and choosing things for their mates has confirmed for me that they are drawn to color. It doesn't have to be a bright red; a soft shade works just as well.

I have countless stories I could tell, but here's a short one that highlights the color concept. A client who was very upset over her waning relationship came to me for some help with dressing for a casual event she and her boyfriend were invited to. She was dreading it and thought it would very likely be their last evening together.

I said, "Let's go for the element of surprise. Because you wear black for the most part, let's try a color." We chose a soft orange cashmere sweater with her favorite jeans - so simple. Her boyfriend couldn't stop complimenting her, not able to keep his hands off her for the entire evening. He didn't know it was the sweater that had renewed his interest. But she did. His attention made her feel terrific and confident. She knew she was showing a much better side of herself. She got the response she desired and started incorporating color into her wardrobe from that evening on. And, yes, their relationship was rekindled."

ADVICE FOR MEN

"You needn't be a fashion model, but something interesting will intrigue her before you even speak. I was so attracted to a guy in a room with at least 15 others because his turquoise leather sneakers caught my eye. He wasn't the most attractive man there, but he got my attention immediately and, the attention of lots of other women in the room, too. For The Party, step it up a bit. Wear something you feel great in, but not your everyday duds. This is a special moment and needs your attention. If you can make it fun, women will pick up on that energy. It will pique their interest because a sense of playfulness is definitely attractive."

♡

15. Sex

This guidebook is about The Party and how to have fun while finding true love. So what, you ask, does that have to do with sex? Everything!

If you meet someone you really like who likes you, too, then what? What is this thing called dating? Do people still date? Or do you immediately hook up and then you're an item? Or are you? When do you become monogamous? What's the protocol these days?

Whatever your age, 20s – 80s, you still participate in your own historical mating ritual if you're conscious of it or not. So, when's the right time to be intimate if you're looking for true love? Just for fun, take a survey of your friends and ask them. I bet you'll hear stories that'll make you laugh.

On their second date, my friend Abigail, 48, was asked by Patrick, 55, "Why don't women want to have sex anymore?"

Patrick had previously been married for twenty-three years. He was surprised by the lack of sex in the new dating world. He remembered being 25 years old and sex being very accessible and casual. Things had changed while he was married. Abigail told him that most women who had been married for a while and were now divorced didn't want to engage in early sex because they didn't want to discover in the 2nd or 3rd month of the relationship that they didn't really like the new guy. Early sex and intimacy confuse things, she told him.

But what if you want to know if you and this new guy are sexually compatible? Since sex is so enjoyable, why not have it with your possible dream guy? Go ahead. Have sex early on. It's exciting. If it works out for you, great. If not, you'll probably decide to wait longer the next time.

Here's what I've taken away from the countless conversations about sex that I've had while researching this guidebook. Wait. Take your time. Waiting a good four to six dates/weeks will never hurt the relationship. If he leaves because he's too impatient, then let him go.

Having sex early on—like the first night or week after meeting—will only cloud things. You may realize a month later that you don't like him as a person, then what? And if he realizes that about you, you may be hurt or even terribly discouraged. Maybe you'll recognize that sex is the only way you two communicate. What if you put on a sexual persona that's not the real you? Lots of young women emulate porn stars because that's what they think young men want. Even porn stars get tired of being in a performance mode all the time. And what about what you need sexually? What then? You may discover you're involved with someone you don't know how to leave.

Relax, if you can. Trust, if you can. Communicate right from the beginning that you want to wait for sex and that getting to know each other, doing things together, and having fun is what you want to experience with him first. Let the sexual chemistry grow. Let the Comfort Chemistry blossom. Let your imagination roam all over his body. Let the wait build the excitement and become part of the courting game. Anticipation itself is an aphrodisiac.

How long do you wait? My therapist suggested six weeks. Six weeks? Whaaat? That's a long time! Remember, you're looking for true love, and not just a hook up. Then, after six weeks, once you've decided that you really do like this person, go for it. Hopefully, it will be worth the wait.

♡

16. Easy to follow step by step directions on throwing The Party

BEFORE THE PARTY

- Read this book, choose to be confident and decide to throw The Party.

- Decide who you'd like to throw it with. Three co-hosts is a good number. But you can certainly do it with one other person or just yourself.

- Pick a date that's two months away. A Saturday evening is the easiest. A Sunday afternoon is another way to go.

- Choose a venue. A house, a party room in a condo complex, a park, a room in a restaurant.

- Come up with an invitation. I've included a few examples. Feel free to create your own. Email or snail mail. Definitely decide on a RSVP date. Expect a few people who've said they'll come to not show up. Expect a few friends of friends who've heard about it to come on their own. Check back three days before the party to make sure you've got all the RSVPs.

- Remember to include in the invitation that men bring food and women bring drinks or vice-versa.

- Check out the menu suggestions in chapter 5 (page 25) if you want to prepare something yourselves.

- Get the sticky nametags and with a magic marker, write out names for The Party Twenty Questions. Have way more than you need because this is a game that can be played throughout the evening.

- Get 4 x 5 cards and write out The Party Fun Questions.

- Decide on the other games for the evening. Choose where in the venue you want each game to be held. Are there enough chairs? How's the lighting? Is there a good area for dancing?

- As the RSVPs come in, keep a list so you'll have a clear idea as to how many people will be attending.

THE NIGHT OF THE PARTY

- Have your co-hosts help you set up your place. Decide on who does what—you all might want to greet your guests with a hug and a slap on the back that attaches the nametag for The Party Twenty Questions game.

- Take a few hours before the party to eat, get dressed and relax. Remember, you want to have a good time, too.

- If you've decided to hire The Party Party Planners, they'll be there to help set up and make sure the party is going well.

DURING THE PARTY

- Take a deep breath. Remember you're doing this to have fun while finding true love. The true love part you have to leave up to chance, destiny and fate. But the fun part is totally up to you!

- Get some phone numbers. Give some phone numbers. Make plans to get together with the people who interest you.

- Have an invitation printed out for a follow-up get together the next weekend – maybe at a bowling alley or a bar. Say on the invitation that anyone wanting to get together again can show up at this bar the following Saturday at 8 PM. It's up to each person if they'd like to meet up. You don't have to show up if you don't want to. You might be surprised at who does come. It's another step in the forward movement of connecting with a group who are like-minded.

- Have fun!

AFTER THE PARTY

- Make sure your co-hosts stay to help clean up. Or you've hired help to clean up.

- Have fun while cleaning up! Talk about everybody. Tell each other things that happened. This is one of the best parts of throwing The Party. Dish while doing the dishes!

- Unwind, take a bath and relax.

- Have a great night sleep. You deserve it!

- Dream about all the possibilities out there.

- Think about whom you'd like to see again. Wait a few days to connect.

- Make connections by calling or texting.
- Decide to throw another Party in a few months. If you follow the steps, you'll meet a whole new group of interesting people who are open to the possibilities of finding true love.

♡

17. The day after

- *What happens if you meet someone you really like?

- *What if you don't meet anyone you like?

- *What if someone likes you, but you don't like them?

- *What if someone you like gives their contact info to your friend, the co-host?

It's time to talk about disappointment. I was going through a rather tough time a few years ago. I'd met some new people when I was opening up my career to include writing and producing. I had meetings and coffee with four different producers who were so positive during our meeting that I was certain the projects were going to move ahead. It turned out that none of these contacts made good on their word. They lied to me by not doing what they promised. I was very saddened by this. I've always been a hopeful person, and this rude behavior really surprised and discouraged me.

I spoke with my therapist about it. I stopped trusting people because I was disappointed in them. She said that if you let experience guide you rather than expectations, you wouldn't be disappointed in life. She explained it this way:

When you know a person for at least three years, you've seen how they behave. You know that if they say they'll be there at 8 PM to pick you up, you can trust them if in the past they've been there at 8 PM to pick you up. An experience with another person will inform you that they'll always be 20 minutes late, no matter what. So, you end up telling them to get to your house at least 20 minutes early because you take into consideration their behavior.

Sarah said you don't know a person's behavior unless you've had time to share experiences with them where their behavior has been displayed. She asked me how long I'd known these producers who had lied to me. I said I didn't really know them at all. I had a few phone calls and one meeting with each of them.

"You've had no experiences with them, no history," she said. "Therefore, you have no idea as to how they'll behave. Having expectations of a person you've had no real experience with will lead to disappointment. The only way not to be disappointed is to reserve any expectations until you know a person."

"Does that mean I can't make a judgment on a person for at least three years?" I asked.

"Three years is when you really know someone. Three months is when you know enough to tell you if you want to continue knowing them," she said. "Try not to make any decisions about someone until you've had some experiences with them. Because if you do, you'll invariably be disappointed."

This advice is not easy to follow. I want to go with my instincts, trust immediately and fall in love quickly. But in truth, I've found her words to be very helpful. I recommend holding back on expectations after The Party. I believe you'll be happier.

♡

18. So why throw The Party, you ask?

You throw The Party because it's an active, creative, playful and empowering thing to do for yourself and others. What I've found to be true is that when I'm embracing those positive actions, good things happen.

You'll create the experience for a room full of openhearted men and women who want to connect with people who also want to find true love. Where else does that exist?

Let me answer the questions from the previous chapter.

What happens if you meet someone you really like?

Feel good that a part of you is excited and interested in someone. As a hostess, you'll probably be able to track them down. Go for it. Try not to have any expectations.

My friend Annabelle, 26, met a guy at one of our parties. She sent him a message on Snapchat and asked him to meet her for a drink. She was nervous because she'd never asked anyone out before. They met at a bar and had a wonderful time. He told her that he was grateful she made the first move because he was too shy and never would've contacted her on his own. They've been together ever since.

WHAT IF YOU DON'T MEET ANYONE YOU LIKE?

Throw another Party. Invite different people. With The Link Effect, you'll meet a whole new group of guests.

WHAT IF SOMEONE LIKES YOU BUT YOU DON'T LIKE HIM OR HER?

Feel flattered. Be honest in a gentle way. Throw another Party.

WHAT IF A GUY YOU LIKE GIVES HIS CONTACT INFO TO YOUR FRIEND, THE CO-HOST?

Be gracious and wish her well. Throw another Party.

♡

19. What I learnt from The Party

My friend, Charlotte, was staying with me. She saw how crazy I got when I had an audition. I was divorced and had started dating, which also made me crazy.

She said, "Look, you probably won't get the part because that's the way your business is. And you probably won't meet your perfect guy because it's a miracle when anybody does, so you might as well go into the audition being exactly who you are and go out on a date the same way. Be yourself. Enjoy the opportunity. And you never know what can happen."

This was some of the best advice ever given to me. I actually followed it. I felt free and excited as compared to anxious and scared. I wasn't concerned anymore about getting the part. Now I focused on my preparation and doing a great audition. I wasn't nervous anymore about going out on a date. I saw dating as a chance to be myself and get to know other people.

Being an actress prepared me for life because almost anything risky can be compared to an audition. Auditions are a lot of work. You have to analyze the script, memorize several pages, dress according to the character, and then compete with many other talented actors for that one role. Auditions are scary. In front of producers, writers and directors (mostly male), you open your heart and soul and deliver a performance that could hopefully change your life, or at least, pay your rent for that month. Getting the part is like winning a lottery. Only one person gets the role. There are no silver medals in acting. Only gold. Getting a part is kind of like a miracle.

I think that's also true in love because it's definitely a miracle when you meet someone you love and who loves you.

Actually, there are miracles everywhere if you look. Einstein said, "There are only two ways to live your life. One is as though nothing is a miracle. The other is as though everything is." Such a beautiful and positive thought.

A caterpillar becoming a butterfly is a miracle. A baby being born is a miracle. A flower blooming is a miracle. Meeting your true love is a miracle. Believe in miracles. I do. It makes life better.

Another very important thing I learnt from throwing The Party is that I can have an idea, think about it, get some support and then make it a reality. The experience of going from concept to fruition is vital when it comes to being responsible for one's life choices.

From co-hosting The Party, my confidence level rose to a 10 out of 10. I can speak to anyone about anything now. I can go up to someone I don't know and say hello and introduce myself. I'm not afraid of anyone's judgment of me. I know that we're all the same down deep because we all want the same things in life - happiness, love, good health, good friends and family and inspiring work. It's when I forget what I know— that's what puts me back a step or two and I revert back to that insecure teenager at her first dance. This is why I wear a red, braided bracelet I call my Remember Who You Are™ bracelet. So when I look at it on my wrist, I stop for a second and actively remember who I am—a worthwhile person who has a lot to contribute—just like you.

Now all I need to remember is to wear it.

20. Did I have fun while finding true love?

You're probably wondering if I met my current husband at The Party and did I have fun? I met him because of The Party and it was a lot of fun. It was The Link Effect. Let me explain.

I auditioned for a guest star role on a TV series and got the part. It shot in San Francisco so I flew up there for a week. At the first read through, I met the writer, Janie. Because of the three Parties I'd thrown, I was relaxed about meeting people, so we got along very well. It wasn't too long before I realized that the character I was playing was a version of her. We laughed a lot on the set and she invited me to have dinner with her the following week when we were back in LA.

At dinner, I met her wonderful standard poodle, Tucker. I asked if I could photograph them, so that weekend, I went over and took fun pictures of Janie and Tucker. She loved the shots, enlarged one to 18" x 20", framed it and hung it on her living room wall.

Janie was friends with a writer. He had dinner at her place (Janie was a great cook) and he admired my photograph. He asked Janie if she thought I could take his picture for the jacket of his new book. Janie said yes, so he made arrangements with his publisher to hire me.

The week before our photo shoot, he called and asked if he could join

Janie and myself in our plans to see a film. I said of course. So, we met that Saturday afternoon. It was pretty much love at first sight for both of us.

Of course, there's a bit more to the story, but the main point I'm making is without the confidence in myself, I don't think I would've so easily connected with Janie and then with her friend. The Link Effect of connecting all the elements, the chain links that came together for us to meet—my confidence from The Party, Charlotte's advice, my ease at being myself, the audition, getting the part, making friends with Janie, taking her photo, her friend admiring the photo, his publisher hiring me to take his picture, and the photo shoot—is how I really met my husband.

And was it fun? Yes! Planning and executing The Parties was a blast. We all laughed so much. I met a lot of interesting people and dated worthy men I never would have met otherwise. I went from being nervous at auditions to really enjoying myself at them. Playing the games at The Party was fantastic. Meeting new people was truly an honor. Everyone has stories you can learn from.

Meeting, getting to know and being with my true love has been one of the happiest periods of my life. What is the secret to our beautiful relationship, you ask? We have great affinity with each other. We laugh and play a lot. We have both Sexual and Comfort Chemistry. I treat him like a king and he treats me like a queen. Perhaps that'll be my next book. I already have the title, *Secrets to a Beautiful Relationship.*

You can't control everything. Actually, on a very deep level, you have no control over anything, so why not trust and plan an event just for the fun of it? You never know, Cupid might be flying around and love may happen. One thing is certain - staying at home waiting for your true love to knock on your door is fine if your true love happens to be the UPS guy. If it's not him, find a co-host or two, get dressed up, have a glass of whatever makes you feel great, and step into the possibility of your better self winning the day. And yes, throw The Party!

♡

21. Love actually...

"Tell me, what is it you plan to do with your one wild and precious life?" wrote the poet Mary Oliver.

When I really ask myself this question, I take a moment to get still. I look inward and whisper, "What is it I plan to do with my one wild and precious life?"

I let thoughts and words tumble out, unedited. I jot them down. I usually come up with an idea or project that brings me a sense of possibility. I like to create—to make things happen that weren't there before. That's why I wrote this book. Doing something proactive is always better than—well, just about anything really. I wrote The Party for Francine, and others who want to have fun while finding true love. And though you don't need a partner to be truly happy, it sure is nice to have someone—a new friend possibly—who cherishes you and thinks you're terrific.

Did everyone who came to The Party meet their true love?

No.

Did everyone who came to The Party have fun?

Yes, if they came with an open mind and heart.

So, go ahead, take a deep breath, and ask yourself what you plan to do with your one wild and precious life. Then listen to your heart answer.

I leave you with these sage words from *Love Actually*, written by Richard Curtis, and spoken by one of my favorite actors, Hugh Grant.

"If you look for it, I've got a sneaky feeling you'll find that love actually is all around."

Have fun and best wishes always,

Terri Hanauer 2024

Photo by Peter Lefcourt

About the author

Terri Hanauer is a multiple award-winning Los Angeles theatre director, most recently winning Broadway World Los Angeles Best Director Award. Her first feature film, Sweet Talk is streaming on Gravitas Films. She directed a season of HBO Cinemax's Zane's Chronicles, and Amazon's Smothered. She is a graduate of AFI's Directing Workshop for Women. She worked extensively as an actress and photographer in the States and Canada appearing on countless TV shows and the Mark Taper Forum and the Arena Stage Theatre. She's a graduate of Toronto's York University with a Bachelor of Fine Arts degree.

Stevie Wonder blessed her baby when she was nine months pregnant, magician Doug Henning hypnotized and sawed her in half when she was his assistant and the hugging saint, Amma, hugged her. She enjoys family, fashion and float tanks. Her debut novel, The Lightness of Rain, will be available this year.

Her friends have always asked her help when it came to relationships so she decided to write *The Party - How To Have Fun While Finding True Love*.

Acknowledgements:

Peter Lefcourt, my partner in all things.
Joan Ryan who was there at the beginning.
Céline Diano and Frédérique Haustête for their present day inspiration.
MK and Jack Grapes for their teaching.
Thaao Penghlis and Efrat Cornfeld for their tasty treats.
Biannti for her style. Biannti@Biannti.Com.
Marlee Novak, Anna Albie and Autumn Marsilio for their thoughts.
C.A. Edwards and Bambi Here for their editing.
Murray Weiss for his belief.
My family and friends for their true love.

ThePartyTheBook.com

Notes